40p

CN01583107

Dictionary Games

illustrated by Tania Hurt-Newton

Contents

Ladybird

Alphabetical order

At Alpha Bet City airport all the check-in desks are in alphabetical order. Some of the signs have fallen down. Fill in the missing signs so that Mark and Maggie March can find out where to check in.

Dave and Daisy Dance have just arrived at the airport. Using the pairs of letters below, circle which check-in desk they will come to first:

m or **f**	**r** or **v**	**g** or **e**	**w** or **s**
n or **q**	**h** or **m**	**d** or **b**	**v** or **i**

The departure gates are also marked alphabetically.
Fill in the letters missing from the signs:

These gate signs have got mixed up. Put them back into alphabetical order. Hurry, Dave and Daisy are waiting to board their flight! The first has been done for you.

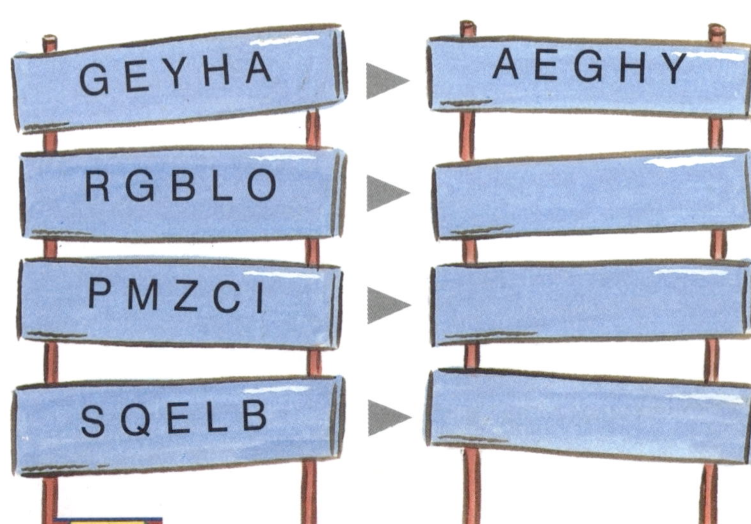

Becky Bell is still packing. She is making lists of things she needs to take on holiday. Help her to put each list into alphabetical order. The first has been done for you.

For the airport

- passport
- tickets
- money
- suitcase
- handbag

- handbag
- money
- passport
- suitcase
- tickets

For the beach

- swimsuit
- towel
- windbreak
- life jacket
- glasses

- ______
- ______
- ______
- ______
- ______

For the theme park

- camera
- hat
- bag
- shorts
- T-shirt

- ______
- ______
- ______
- ______
- ______

For long walks

- boots
- socks
- knapsack
- jacket
- map

- ______
- ______
- ______
- ______
- ______

When you put words into alphabetical order, words beginning with **a** come first, **b** next, and so on, ending with words beginning with **z**.

Alphabet challenge

How quickly can you say the alphabet?

How quickly can you say it backwards?

Alphabetising by second letter

On the way to the airport, Ben Bell saw:

family **fe**nce **fi**re **fl**owers **fo**untain

Sort these lists of other things Ben and Becky Bell saw on the way to the airport by looking at the second letter of each one. If you get it right, the words will fit in the grids!

minibus
market

mosque
museum
memorial

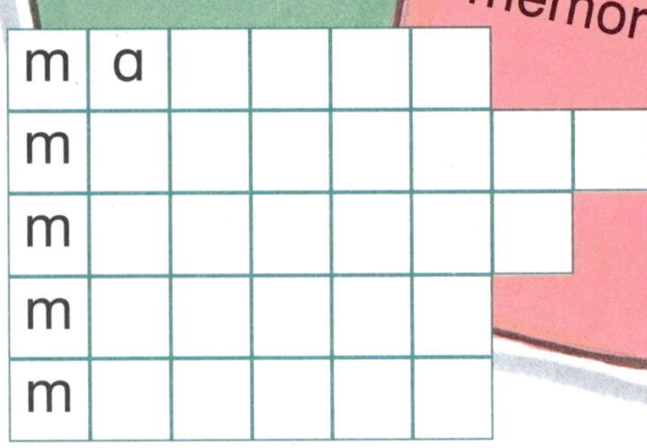

garage
golf club

gymnasium
greenhouse
guesthouse

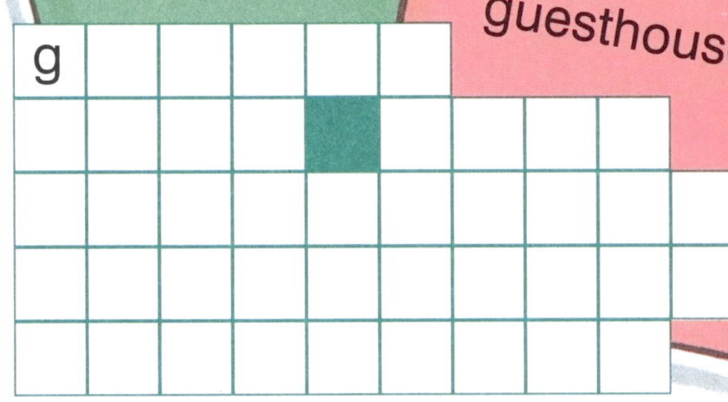

At the airport they checked the departure and arrival boards to see if their flight was on time. Sort the cities into alphabetical order.

Departures
Seoul
Sydney

Sheffield
Salzburg
Stockholm

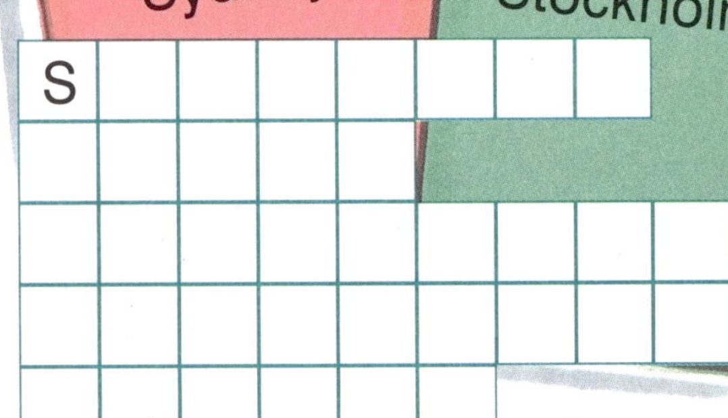

Arrivals
Berlin
Boston

Brussels
Bangkok
Budapest

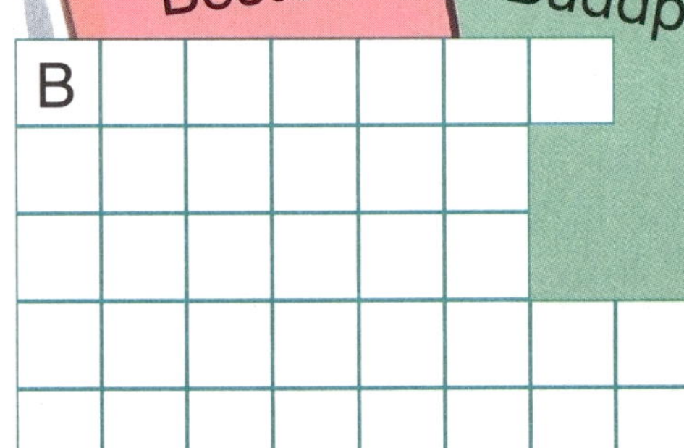

Daisy and Dave Dance played the **Dictionary Challenge Game** on the plane. You will need a dictionary to play with them.

Look in your dictionary to find the first word that begins with **c**.

Write it here:

Now find the last word beginning with **c**.

Write it here:

Use your dictionary to find the first and last words for the following letters.

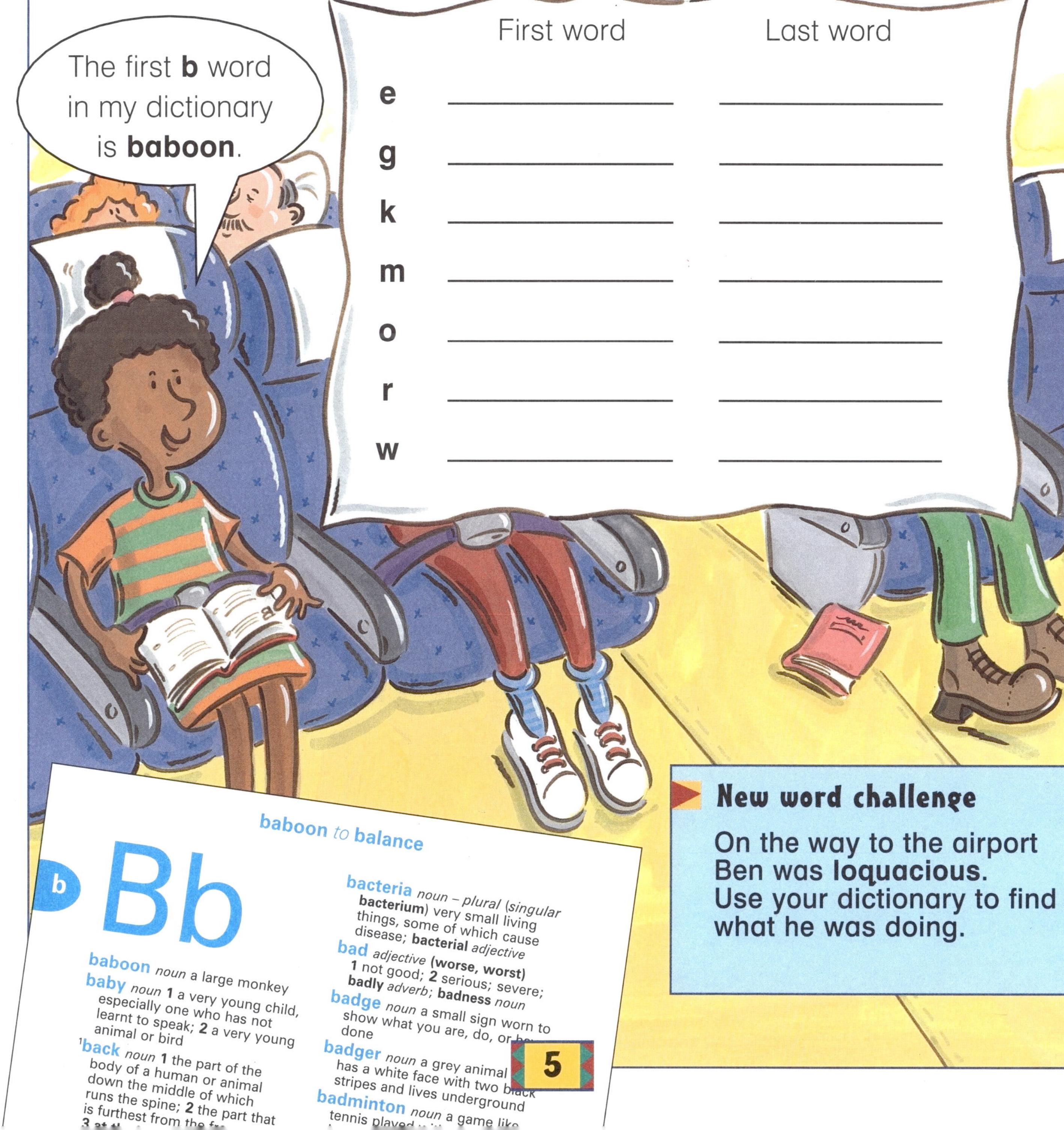

	First word	Last word
e	________	________
g	________	________
k	________	________
m	________	________
o	________	________
r	________	________
w	________	________

New word challenge

On the way to the airport Ben was **loquacious.**
Use your dictionary to find out what he was doing.

Staircases

The families need to climb up lots of stairs to reach their hotel. Help them by filling in the missing words on this staircase. Use your dictionary to check your answers.

1. You put it on with a brush to colour something
2. A juicy fruit with a furry skin
3. A small pool of rainwater
4. A man, woman or child
5. A black and white bird with webbed feet
6. To own or have
7. A breakfast cereal with oats

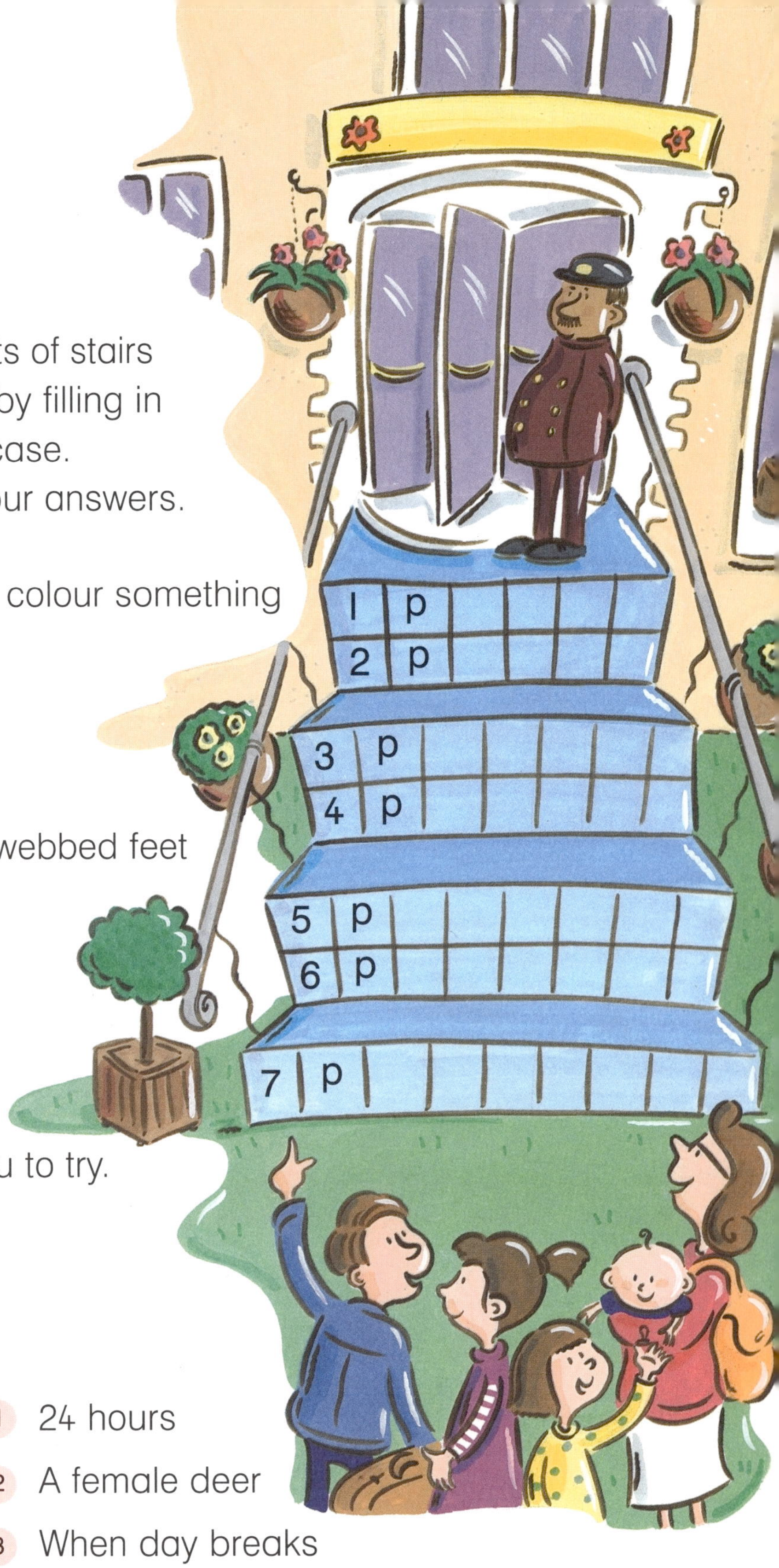

Here's another staircase for you to try.

1. 24 hours
2. A female deer
3. When day breaks
4. A musical instrument played by beating
5. A place for dancing
6. A small wild flower with white petals
7. To do harm to things

The hotel receptionist will not check any of the families in until their suitcases are in alphabetical order, by person's name. Help them to put the names in the right order.

Third letter challenge

Complete the grid to find out what direction the plane flew in when it took the families on holiday. Use a dictionary to check your answers. When the grid is complete the direction will appear in the white boxes.

1. **You smell with this**
2. **A Chinese food rather like spaghetti**
3. **Not anywhere**
4. **To try to do something**
5. **Nothing or zero**

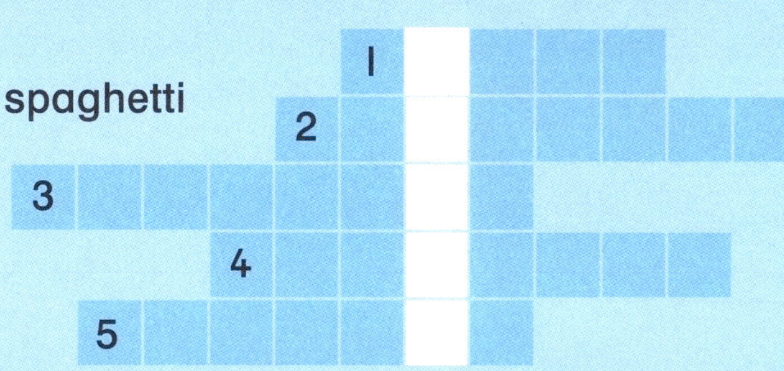

The plane flew _ _ _ _ _ .

Find the meaning

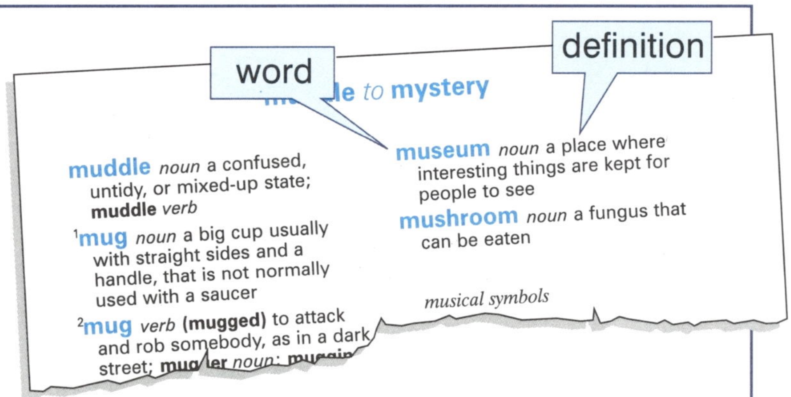

Using your dictionary to help, draw a line to connect the words to the correct definitions. The first has been done for you.

1 A salt-water lake separated from the sea

2 A place where interesting things are kept for people to see

3 A place where food is bought and eaten

museum

ca____

aqu_____

re_________

ca__

la____

4 A tunnel or hole in a cliff or underground

5 A large building built to withstand enemy attacks

6 A place where many kinds of fish and other water creatures are kept

The March family went to the Water Sports Centre.
What can they do or see there?
Check your answers using a dictionary.

1 s _ _ _
To move through water using your arms and legs

2 d _ _ _
To jump head first into the water

3 c _ _ _ _
A light narrow boat that you paddle

4 d _ _ _ _ _
A small boat for rowing or sailing

5 s _ _ _
To travel in a boat that uses wind power

6 j _ _ _
To move your body quickly and suddenly into the air

7 r _ _
To move through the water with oars

8 f _ _ _ _
To stay on top of the water without sinking

Water sport challenge

Fit the words into the grid to find another water sport.

What is the word in the white boxes?

Look it up in your dictionary and write what it means here: ____________________

____

____

Technology museum

The Dance family went to the Technology Museum. Daisy and Dan liked the robot room. Some of the labels on the robot are missing. Help them to fill in the missing letters.

One of the rooms in the museum had lots of model buildings. Can you work out what buildings Daisy and Dan saw by solving this puzzle?

1 A place where you go to learn
2 A place where criminals are kept
3 Where things are made
4 An old building surrounded by a moat
5 The house of a king or queen
6 You keep the car in here
7 A place to stay where you must pay for your room and meals

What is the building in the white boxes? ____________________

Museum challenge

Hidden in this word search are some of the things which the Dance family saw at the Technology Museum. Can you find them all? The clues will help.

A piece of equipment designed to do a particular job

A wheel with teeth which turns another wheel or part

A machine used for powering spacecraft

A piece of metal that can pull iron towards it

The front surface of a television

A machine that uses fuel to make something move

m	a	c	h	i	n	e
p	b	o	g	d	q	n
m	a	g	n	e	t	g
r	o	c	k	e	t	i
y	p	r	a	c	x	n
s	c	r	e	e	n	e

Use your dictionary

Try Ben's puzzle. It is in two parts. First you need to find the missing words. Use your dictionary to help. If the male word is given, then find the female word. If the female is given, fill in the male.

Male	Female
drake	________
gander	________
________	vixen
son	________
________	niece
________	aunt
duke	________
________	princess
king	________
________	actress

On a separate sheet of paper rearrange the ten new words you've found into alphabetical order to solve Ben's puzzle.

Take
the 1st letter of the 8th word
the last letter of the 10th word
the 2nd letter of the 2nd word
the 4th letter of the 7th word
the last two letters of the 9th word

The answer is the female word for a peacock: ________

four *to* **front**

four *adjective, noun* the number 4; **fourth** *adjective, adverb* (*see last page*); • **for, fore**

fourteen *adjective, noun* the number 14; **fourteenth** *adjective, adverb* (*see last page*)

fox *noun* (*female* **vixen**, *young* **cub**) a small wild animal like a dog, with a bushy tail and reddish fur

fraction *noun* a very small piece or amount; a part of a whole number ($\frac{2}{3}$, $\frac{7}{16}$, etc)

frame *noun* **1** the rods and bars which are fitted together to make something or round which something is built: **framework**; **2** the pieces of wood, plastic, or metal round a picture; **frame** *verb*

free *adjective* **1** able to do what you like; not tied up or in prison; **2** not costing …

… supplied; **4** not preserved in tins, bottles, etc; not frozen; **5** clean or pure; **6** not tired; healthy; **freshness** *noun*; **freshly** *adverb*

Friday *noun* the sixth day of the week

fridge a machine in which food and drinks can be kept cool

friend *noun* a person you like and enjoy talking to and going out with; somebody who is kind and helpful; **friendliness** *noun*; **friendly** *adjective*; **friendship** *noun*

frighten *verb* to make somebody afraid

fro *see* TO AND FRO

frog *noun* a small animal that can live in water and on land and has long …

The plurals for these words are hidden in the wordsearch. Use your dictionary to help Becky find them.

Plural means that there are **more than one**.

man ____________

woman ____________

shelf ____________

ox ____________

potato ____________

foot ____________

baby ____________

tooth ____________

lady ____________

leaf ____________

family ____________

wife ____________

o	s	h	e	l	v	e	s	h	f
l	e	a	v	e	s	p	q	w	a
b	a	c	d	l	f	o	g	i	m
u	n	d	f	e	e	t	i	v	i
o	t	l	i	g	m	a	b	e	l
x	t	p	p	e	f	t	a	s	i
e	m	e	n	e	s	o	b	g	e
n	i	s	h	q	x	e	i	o	s
y	w	o	m	e	n	s	e	o	e
t	e	e	t	h	o	t	s	s	l

Plural challenge

Can you work out which of the plural words fit into these sentences?

Becky's ____________ gleamed when she smiled.

Maggie bought a plant with red and green ____________.

Ben got his ________ wet when he walked along the beach.

Bernie and Matt didn't go swimming because they are too young. They are still __________ .

Food, glorious food

The March family are in the restaurant. The menu is all mixed up. Use your dictionary to help them sort it out. One has already been done for you.

Main courses

curry	small pieces of meat and vegetables grilled on a skewer
kebab	a tortilla that is folded and then filled
hot pot	squid
taco	a lamb, beef or mutton stew
calamary	a spicy dish of vegetables, meat or fish, often served with rice

Vegetables

radish	a kind of chicory with red leaves
artichoke	a dark green leafy vegetable
spinach	an edible flower head
kohlrabi	a small round salad vegetable with a strong taste
radicchio	a kind of cabbage with a turnip-shaped stem

Sweets

custard	a piece of pastry filled with jam or fruit
ice cream	a frozen dessert made from fruit juice and egg whites
sorbet	a yellow sauce often served with puddings
tart	a light sweet containing cream or egg whites
mousse	a creamy frozen dessert

If the word isn't in your dictionary, try looking in another one.

Can you work out what Mark had to drink?

Maggie decided to have fruit instead of a sweet. The fruit she chose is in the white boxes.

1. A big juicy fruit with lots of seeds. Usually cut into slices
2. A juicy fruit that is narrower at the top and rhymes with bear
3. A long yellow fruit that is easy to peel
4. A sour fruit which is good in drinks
5. This fruit is small and grows in bunches. It can be green or black
6. A furry fruit full of juice, with a big stone

What fruit did Maggie have?

____

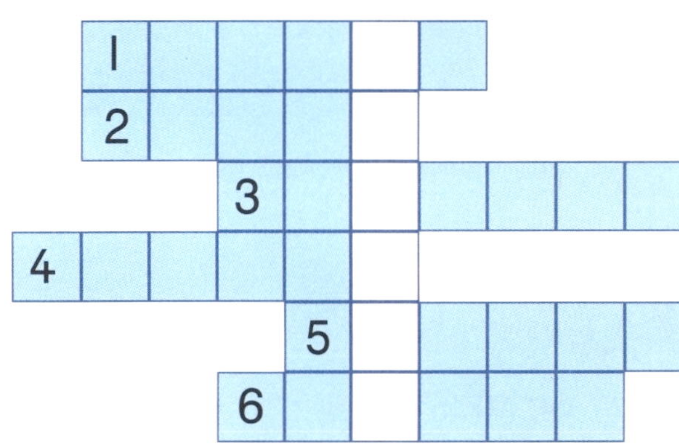

Food challenge

Find a food word in the dictionary and tell your friend what it means (without saying the word). You could give a hint, for example: it starts with a p and has five letters. Your friend needs to find the food word in the dictionary. Take turns.

The zoo

The Bell family saw lots of different animals when they went to the zoo. Use your dictionary to find out the answers to these animal questions.

Answer **yes** or **no**

Can an otter swim? ________

Do monkeys have tails? ________

Do snakes have legs? ________

Does a leopard have stripes? ________

Is an eel a fish? ________

Where do these animals come from?

giraffe ________

llama ________

emu ________

ostrich ________

giant panda ________

Can you answer these animal questions?

What does a mongoose fight? ________

What is a mule a cross between? ________

Are penguins found in the Arctic? ________

What do aardvarks eat? ________

Is a wren large or small? ________

What does a vulture eat? ________

The letters OKDNYE can be rearranged to make the word DONKEY.

The letters in these words are all mixed up. Rearrange them to find out the animals. The clues will help.

ykmneo – a long-tailed tree-climbing animal

_ _ _ _ _ _

ilno – a large wild animal from the cat family

_ _ _ _

yoje – a young kangaroo

_ _ _ _

umiptpoohpas – a large animal with a thick skin that lives near water

_ _ _ _ _ _ _ _ _ _ _ _

rqiersul – a small animal with a bushy tail

_ _ _ _ _ _ _ _

aceml – a large animal with one or two humps

_ _ _ _ _

tnheepla – a large animal with two curved tusks and a long trunk

_ _ _ _ _ _ _ _

ujgara – a large spotted member of the cat family

_ _ _ _ _ _

Animal challenge

On a separate sheet of paper rearrange the words into alphabetical order.

Take
the last letter of the 2nd word
the 2nd letter of the 6th word
the 3rd letter of the 4th word
the 4th letter of the 1st word
the 5th letter of the last word

What animal do you get?

_ _ _ _ _

Homophones and rhymes

Read this story about the Dance family's day out. Use your dictionary to work out which is the correct homophone in each sentence. Circle the correct word.

There was still **dew**/**due** on the grass when the Dance family got up.

"Lets go to the **beech**/**beach**," said the children.

On the way Darren stubbed his **toe**/**tow**.

He felt a **pane**/**pain** go up his leg.

He soon forgot it when he saw the **see**/**sea**.

Daisy and Mrs Dance went for a **sale**/**sail** round the bay.

Mr Dance lay under the parasol and was **idol**/**idle** all day.

David won a sandcastle competition and was given a **medal**/**meddle**.

"It's been a **great**/**grate** day," said Mrs Dance as they walked back to the hotel.

Circle the words that rhyme in this poem:

Daisy Dance liked to play
on the beach, every day.
She told the clouds, "If you may,
please do stay far away."

Use your dictionary to help you complete this rhyming puzzle.

Across

2 Begins with **f** and rhymes with **hive**

3 Begins with **p** and rhymes with **match**

5 Begins with **m** and rhymes with **petal**

6 Begins with **l** and rhymes with **bend**

Down

1 Begins with **n** and rhymes with **fight**

3 Begins with **p** and rhymes with **stool**

4 Begins with **c** and rhymes with **take**

New word challenge

Damien was surprised that the sea was **saline**. Use your dictionary to find out what this means.

Parts of speech

Think of one word to fit into each sentence about the March family's trip to the playground. Look in a dictionary to check it is the right part of speech.

Maggie wanted to go on the ________________.

Noun (n)

A noun names someone or something.

She climbed up the ________________ ladder.

Adjective (adj)

An adjective tells us more about a noun.

________________ closed her eyes when she went down.

Pronoun (pro)

A pronoun is used instead of a noun.

Mark ________________ Matt on the swings.

Verb (vb)

A verb is a being or doing word.

Matt is a baby, so Mark had to push ________________

Adverb (adv)

An adverb tells us more about a verb. It tells us how, when or where the action of a verb happens.

Mabel crawled ________________ the climbing frame.

Preposition (prep)

A preposition tells us the position of something.

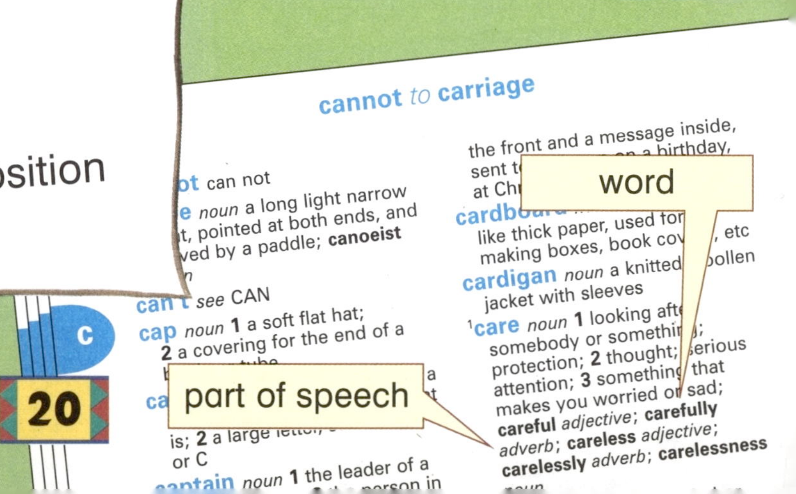

The children are ready for ice cream. Use your dictionary to fill their cones with interesting words. Fill each cone with the correct parts of speech.

Ice cream challenge

Some words can be used in more than one way and can fit into more than one cone. How many words like this can you find?

One word, two or more meanings

Some of the words in this story have more than one meaning. Which is the correct definition of the word in **bold** in each sentence.

1 The Dance family went to the **fair**.

(a) honest and reasonable

(b) a large market with amusements

2 Dan tried the first stall. He needed to throw **flat** hoops over the bottle tops to win.

(a) smooth, having no bumps

(b) dull, uninteresting

3 With his first two hoops Dan **missed** the bottle tops.

(a) felt sad because someone wasn't with him

(b) failed to reach

4 "You need to hold your hand **steady**," the stall holder said.

(a) dependable

(b) not moving or changing

5 "This time the hoop will **fit**," said Dan. He tried again, and it did!

(a) go into place

(b) in good health

6 Daisy played a game where you had to **fire** a gun to hit the number cards.

(a) shoot a bullet from a gun

(b) bake clay in a kiln or oven

7 Every time the gun went off it made a **bang**.

(a) heavy blow

(b) sudden loud noise

8 She had to get a **score** of over ten to win a prize.

(a) how many points made in a game

(b) twenty

9 Daisy scored twelve so she won some large fluffy **dice**.

(a) to cut something up small

(b) cubes with dots on each of their six faces

Meaning challenge

Some of the words written in bold have more than two meanings. Look them up in your dictionary to see how many other definitions you can find. What is the greatest number of meanings that you can find for one word?

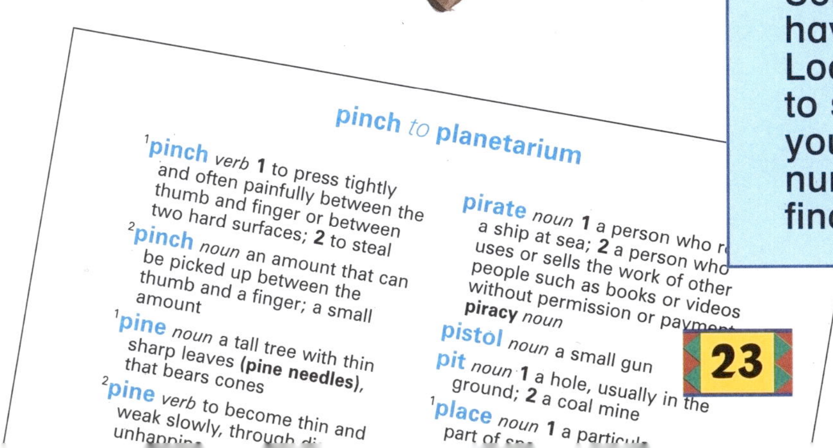

pinch *to* planetarium

[1]**pinch** *verb* **1** to press tightly and often painfully between the thumb and finger or between two hard surfaces; **2** to steal

[2]**pinch** *noun* an amount that can be picked up between the thumb and a finger; a small amount

[1]**pine** *noun* a tall tree with thin sharp leaves **(pine needles)**, that bears cones

[2]**pine** *verb* to become thin and weak slowly, through di… unhappin…

pirate *noun* **1** a person who r… a ship at sea; **2** a person who uses or sells the work of other people such as books or videos without permission or payment **piracy** *noun*

pistol *noun* a small gun

pit *noun* **1** a hole, usually in the ground; **2** a coal mine

[1]**place** *noun* **1** a particul… part of sp…

Answers

PAGE 2

a**b**c**de**f**g**hij**k**lm**n**op**q**r**s**tuv**w**x**y**z

f, r, e, s, n, h, b, i

DEF**GH**IJKL**MN**, P**QR**STUVW**XYZ**

BGLOR, CIMPZ, BELQS

PAGE 3

glasses, life jacket, swimsuit, towel, windbreak

bag, camera, hat, shorts, T-shirt

boots, jacket, knapsack, map, socks

PAGE 4

market, memorial, minibus, mosque, museum

garage, golf club, greenhouse, guesthouse, gymnasium

Salzburg, Seoul, Sheffield, Stockholm, Sydney

Bangkok, Berlin, Boston, Brussels, Budapest

PAGE 6

1 paint **2** peach **3** puddle **4** person **5** penguin **6** possess **7** porridge

1 day **2** doe **3** dawn **4** drum **5** disco **6** daisy **7** damage

PAGE 7

Daisy, Damien, Dan, Darren, Dave

Becky, Belinda, Ben, Bernie, Betty

Mabel, Maggie, Mandy, Mark, Matt

1 nose **2** noodles **3** nowhere **4** attempt **5** nought

The plane flew – **north**

PAGE 8

1 lagoon **3** restaurant **4** cave **5** castle **6** aquarium

PAGE 9

1 swim **2** dive **3** canoe **4** dinghy **5** sail **6** jump **7** row **8** float

windsurf – to ride over the water on a board with a sail

PAGE 10

eye, ear, mouth, chin, wrist, hand, thigh, knee, ankle, toe, eyebrow, nose, neck, thumb, finger, elbow, chest, shin, heel

PAGE 11

1 school **2** prison **3** factory **4** castle **5** palace **6** garage **7** hotel

cottage

m	a	c	h	i	n	e
p	b	o	g	d	q	n
m	a	g	n	e	t	g
r	o	c	k	e	t	i
y	p	r	a	c	x	n
s	c	r	e	e	n	e

PAGE 12

drake – duck, gander – goose, fox – vixen, son – daughter, nephew – niece, uncle – aunt, duke – duchess, prince – princess, king – queen, actor – actress

peahen

PAGE 13

men, women, shelves, oxen, potatoes, feet, babies, teeth, ladies, leaves, families, wives

Plural challenge

teeth, leaves, feet, babies

o	s	h	e	l	v	e	s	h	f
l	e	a	v	e	s	p	q	w	a
b	a	c	d	l	f	o	g	i	m
u	n	d	f	e	e	t	i	v	i
o	t	l	i	g	m	a	b	e	l
x	t	p	p	e	f	t	a	s	i
e	m	e	n	e	s	o	b	g	e
n	i	s	h	q	x	e	i	o	s
y	w	o	m	e	n	s	e	o	e
t	e	e	t	h	o	t	s	s	l

PAGE 14

Main courses

curry – a spicy dish of vegetables, meat or fish...

kebab – small pieces of meat... on a skewer

hot pot – a lamb, beef or mutton stew

taco – a tortilla that is folded and then filled

calamary – squid

Vegetables

radish – a small round salad vegetable...

artichoke – an edible flower head

spinach – a dark green leafy vegetable

kohlrabi – a kind of cabbage...

radicchio – a kind of chicory with red leaves

Sweets

custard – a yellow sauce often served with puddings

ice cream – a creamy frozen dessert

sorbet – a frozen dessert made from fruit juice...

tart – a piece of pastry filled with jam or fruit

mousse – a light sweet containing cream...

PAGE 15

lemonade

1 melon **2** pear **3** banana **4** lemon **5** grape **6** peach

orange

PAGE 16

yes, yes, no, no, yes

Africa, South America, Australia, Africa, China

snakes, a horse and a donkey, no, ants and termites, a wren is small, dead animals

PAGE 17

monkey, joey, squirrel, elephant, jaguar, lion, hippopotamus, camel

tiger

PAGE 18

1 dew **2** beach **3** toe **4** pain **5** sea **6** sail **7** idle **8** medal **9** great

PAGE 19

play, day, may, stay, away

Across **2** five **3** patch **5** metal **6** lend

Down **1** night **3** pool **4** cake

PAGE 22

1 (b) **2** (a) **3** (b) **4** (b) **5** (a)

PAGE 23

6 (a) **7** (b) **8** (a) **9** (b)